Dedicated

to my husband Augustin

and

to my daughter Shyian

Table of Contents

Foreword

About the Author

Simone St. Fort is a wife of 36-years and a mother of one. She is presently the full-time pastor at the Deniere Riviere Joyful Assembly, St. Lucia. She was born and raised in the church community. Her ministry involves teaching, preaching, and counseling; especially on issues related to marriage and family.

She holds a Master's Degree in Theology and Counseling, a Bachelor's in Education (U.W.I.) and a Master's Degree in Educational Administration (Leicester University). She is also almost finished completing a Doctorate in Divinity of Counseling. She served as a teacher for twenty-eight (28) years and a principal for sixteen (16); retiring from her full-time job in 2017. She is also the founder and president of the "Hope for Marriages" ministry. She offers counsel and hosts workshops and seminars for many married couples and single individuals, nationwide.

Simone St. Fort is also the founder and president of the "Bridge of Hope Community" foundation, which caters to the needs of the marginalized, underprivileged and vulnerable women in society through skills and educational training.

The church has become a place where only 20% of believers are fulfilling the call of God in their lives. Sadly, too many believers don't even know what their call is! In 2016 the Lord gave me a vision of the urgency for His people to be engaged in Kingdom building. He gave me the theme *Servanthood* as we are called to serve the Kingdom with our all. This book draws on biblical examples to help motivate believers to discover their God-given call and for those who have discovered it, to follow it to completion.

Like Jesus, we were all brought into the Kingdom to serve and not to be served. As a member of the Body of Christ, we must thus function as the part we were created to be. As a non-functional body part affects our entire body, members who are not functioning are hindering the entire Body of Christ from going forward. No one else can do what you were saved to do! At the end of your life, you will be asked to give an account to God, so it is my desire that we all work together until He returns. Do not be found guilty of impeding the Body when you stand before your Master!

Introduction

The title of this book, "Servanthood," came from a vision given to me by God in the year 2016. It is a theme God gave me for our local church but entrusted me to share so that believers can work while it is day, before the night comes when no man can work. Consequently, I began writing with one main objective in mind: to motivate believers to use their spiritual gifts zealously, with the power of God, to edify the church.

This book promises to be an enlightening one! I aim to accomplish the will of God in this season, by encouraging the believers to know and operate in their purpose and calling. I want to help you go through the process of discovering and developing your spiritual gifts for the honor and glory of God. My desire is for an awakening of the Holy Spirit in the lives of believers so that they can become more effective as opposed to the normal dry theological exercise we see happening every day.

I pray that you will grow through this book and be used tremendously in your local assembly. Some of you may have started doing the will of God in your life and I admonish you to continue and beseech God to use you more. Some of you may have started well but got derailed along the way; I admonish you to pick it up again. Some of you may have not yet started and I assure you like Esther and Joseph that you were born for such a time as this. Be courageous and start now; it is your time and your season to finish what you were created for – the specific assignment that God has given to you.

Some of you may not be sure at all what your particular task is, so I pray as you read through these pages that God will reveal it to you. Let us mobilize each other to complete all our God-given responsibilities on this earth. As the songwriter says, "Lord don't let me leave behind an unfinished task." I want to end with this reminder that the highest position in God's Kingdom is to be a servant to all. May God continue to be praised and glorified in all that He has begun and what He will do in each life! Be engaged until He comes!

Chapter One
A Call to Servanthood

God has been calling His people "servant" since the olden days. Isaiah 44:21 states, "Remember these things, O Jacob, And Israel, for you are My servant; I have formed you, you are My servant, O Israel, you will not be forgotten by Me." Psalms 89:3 says, "I have made a covenant with My chosen; I have sworn to David My servant." The word servant means slave, but it also refers to a place of order. The two terms are often used interchangeably. If there is a difference, it is usually one suitable to the context in which it is being used. "Slave" may be used for a person in relation to his master, but "servant" in relation to his work. "Slave" may be in the context of submission to a superior, whereas "servant" is in the context of service to others.

Likewise, this concept has been reiterated in the New Testament. Romans 6:16-18 says, "Do you not know that when you present yourselves to someone as slaves for obedience, you are slaves of the one whom you obey, either of sin resulting in death, or of obedience resulting in righteousness? But thanks be to God that though you were slaves of sin, you became obedient from the heart to that form of teaching to which you were committed, and having been freed from sin, you became slaves of righteousness." Also, Ephesians 6:6 declares, "not by way of eye service, as men-pleasers, but as slaves of Christ, doing the will of God from the heart." 1Corinthians 4:1 adds, "Let a man regard us in this manner, as servants of Christ and stewards of the mysteries of God."

Therefore, we realize that Christians are both slaves and servants of our Lord. What about you? We are called to serve one another, such as in Galatians 5:13 which tells us, "For you were called to freedom, brethren; only *do* not *turn* your freedom into an opportunity for the flesh, but through love serve one another." Also, in Philippians 2:5-7, "Have this attitude in yourselves which was also in Christ Jesus, who, although He existed in the form of God, did not regard equality with God a thing to be grasped, but emptied Himself, taking the form of a bond-servant, and being made in the likeness of men."

Jesus Christ literally emptied Himself, not by giving up His deity, but by laying aside His glory and submitting to the humiliation of becoming a man. He put aside His position and glory of divinity and took on the nature of a servant. This is what Paul was emphasizing to the Corinthians when he said, "For you know the grace of our Lord Jesus Christ that though He was rich, yet for your sake, He became poor so that you through His poverty might become rich." (2Corinthians 8:9).

In Matthew 20:26-28, Jesus beautifully illustrates the true meaning of servanthood when He says, "It is not this way among you, but whoever wishes to become great among you shall be your servant, and whoever wishes to be first among you shall be your slave; just as the Son of Man did not come to be served, but to serve, and to give His life a ransom for many." Oh, how I wish some of us would really get it! When you become a Christian, because you are a servant, you don't just sit or stand and allow others to serve you. Then what is your role? We must have the attitude of Christ by asking, "In what capacity can I serve?"

Picture yourself getting a call to begin an incredible career opportunity where the pay is right, the co-workers are wonderful to work with, the benefits are unbelievable, and the retirement package is really, out of this world. Wow! You send in your application and you are hired. What a thrilling moment it would be! Are we as Christians answering the call of God with such enthusiasm? When you really understand why you have been called by God and you begin to serve the Lord of Lords, the King of Kings, and the Creator of every work or job, then you will also know that the service of God is an exciting adventure, surpassing anything man has ever devised.

Unfortunately, in the secular realm, just about 20% of the employees do 80% of the work and much work plain goes undone. Sound familiar? If you are part of the 20%, because you believe in the hard work and success, you keep on going and going until sometimes you get burnt out. Sad to say, many Christians are in the same boat when it comes to the work of God. We are saved but we do very little or nothing at all with the tools God has given to us. We keep on asking a number of questions, expecting to be answered by the 20% of workers- Where is the usher? Why aren't the toilets clean? Why is the church not cleaned? Where is the bus driver? When last was cell meeting held? Who is responsible for this activity? The list goes on! We are satisfied to be served by the handful.

There is still an underlying problem in the Body of Christ! Some people never accomplish much in serving the Lord because they are not willing to do the small things. They may be happy to stand behind the pulpit but will not consider being a cleaner or usher. They prefer the reward of man's acclamation more than just pleasing God. The great Evangelist D.L. Moody said, "The reward of service is…more service." This is another reason why the 20% end up doing the bulk of the work. In John 13:13-17 Jesus gave a great example of servanthood, "You call Me Teacher and Lord; and you are right, for *so* I am. If I then, the Lord and the Teacher, washed your feet, you also ought to wash one another's feet. For I gave you an example that you also should do as I did to you.

Truly, truly, I say to you, a slave is not greater than his master, nor *is* one who is sent greater than the one who sent him."

Jesus performed a menial task to show that although He was both a teacher and a master, He was still a servant to His people. He stooped so low as to wash their feet, the lowest part of the body and so it should be the same among us. No service should be too low for us to perform for each other. It doesn't matter what title you carry, be it apostle, doctor, bishop or simply brother or sister, our position can never be greater than Jesus'. John testifies and said, "*It is* He who comes after me, the thong of whose sandal I am not worthy to untie," (John 1:27). There is yet a fundamental truth in the example Jesus laid. In the same book of the Bible, it says, "Then He poured water into the basin, and began to wash the disciples' feet and to wipe them with the towel with which He was girded," (John 13:5). This lowly task is usually performed by a servant, but Jesus did it to demonstrate selfless service in its truest sense.

We can never serve too much or serve only in altar ministry. Yes, it is possible for you to be a pastor and at the moment a service presents itself, you believe it is not part of your job, so you leave it undone. But this is not servanthood! I hope you are understanding the extent of servanthood. Jesus did it all the way! But wait, even the disciples had a great misconception of servanthood. Even after Jesus spoke and demonstrated to them, He had to rebuke them. Luke 22:25-27 declares, "And He said to them, "The kings of the Gentiles lord it over them; and those who have authority over them are called 'Benefactors.' But *it is* not this way with you, but the one who is the greatest among you must become like the youngest, and the leader like the servant. For who is greater, the one who reclines *at the table* or the one who serves? Is it not the one who reclines *at the table*? But I am among you as the one who serves."

What's the conclusion? Christians are called to serve just as Christ came, not to be served, but to serve.

Servant of God

In the Old Testament, God referred to many of His followers as servants:

1) Abraham – "The Lord appeared to him the same night and said, "I am the God of your father Abraham; do not fear, for I am with you. I will bless you, and multiply your descendants, For the sake of My servant Abraham." (Genesis 26:24)

2) Moses – "When Israel saw the great power which the Lord had used against the Egyptians, the people feared the Lord, and they believed in the Lord and in His servant Moses." (Exodus 14:31)

3) Caleb – "But My servant Caleb, because he has had a different spirit and has followed Me fully, I will bring into the land which he entered, and his descendants shall take possession of it." (Numbers 14:24)

4) Samuel – "And Eli said to Samuel, "Go lie down, and it shall be if He calls you, that you

shall say, 'Speak, Lord, for Your servant is listening.'" So, Samuel went and lay down in his place." (1Samuel 3:9)

Jesus as a Servant

Jesus found much pleasure in doing the will of His Father. When He was 12 years of age, His mother was out looking for Him because He slipped away from her. He was found in the temple, reasoning with the elders there. His mother went to question Him concerning His whereabouts and He said to her that He came on this earth to do His Father's will. His mission was to do whatever He left heaven to do and He didn't waste time in fulfilling such. He said in John 6:38, "For I have come down from heaven, not to do My own will, but the will of Him who sent Me." John 17:4 says, "I glorified You on the earth, having accomplished the work which You have given Me to do." Jesus very frequently would remind His followers that He came to be a servant to His Father, and we know that He did it with honor. Let us do the same, as Jesus' servants, serve Him with honor!

Chapter Two
Know Your Calling

Have you found your area of service? Are you functioning in it? Every Christian is called to serve and should be delighted to do so. The good thing about it is that the services have been outlined in the Scriptures. Let us look at what the Bible says about services or what is referred to as spiritual gifting.

1Corinthians 12:4-5 says, "Now there are varieties of gifts, but the same Spirit. And there are varieties of ministries, and the same Lord." God has distributed various gifts because He knows our needs. In order for us to grow into perfection, each individual needs a number of services offered to them. In Ephesians 4:11-13 it says, "And He gave some as apostles, and some as prophets, and some as evangelists, and some as pastors and teachers, for the equipping of the saints for the work of service, to the building up of the body of Christ; until we all attain to the unity of the faith, and of the knowledge of the Son of God, to a mature man, to the measure of the stature which belongs to the fullness of Christ."

Why did He distribute the gifts? 1) to equip the saints for the work of the ministry, and 2) to encourage the Body of Christ. In essence, the gifts equip the saints, then the saints serve and as a result, the Body is built up. The gifts named in Ephesians 4:11 are known as the Five-Fold Ministry. These were given to cause the followers of Jesus to work together effectively. Its goal is to train, equip and prepare the Body of Christ to be functional in everyday life and in the ministry of the gospel of Jesus Christ. In short, the Five-Fold Ministry edifies, unifies, prepares, reconciles and molds the Body of Christ. In this way, the Body of Christ grows and expands numerically and spiritually.

So, we realize when we don't carry out our Christian service, we stifle the Body of Christ and stunt the growth of the church. Also, in Ephesians 4:13 Paul made it plain that the work of the ministry should continue until the coming of the Lord. Presently, as the Body, we have not attained the fullness Paul speaks about in that verse. Christians still have different views on many things but at the end of it all, there should be one understanding. However, we must always try to equip and encourage the Body. In the absence of that, the Body would be immature, unstable and gullible, moving to and fro to every wind of doctrine as Ephesians 4:14-15 states.

Let us look at 1Corinthians 12:8-11 where Paul mentions a number of different gifts, all given by God through the Holy Spirit, "For to one is given the word of wisdom through the Spirit, and to another the word of knowledge according to the same Spirit; to another faith by the same Spirit, and to another gifts of healing by the one Spirit, and to another the effecting of miracles, and to another prophecy, and to another the distinguishing of spirits, to another *various* kinds of tongues, and to another the interpretation of tongues. But one and the same Spirit works all these things, distributing to each one individually just as He wills."

Here we see nine (9) gifts being revealed:

A. Gifts of Inspiration (Speaking)

   i.   Speaking in Tongues

   II.   Interpretation of Tongues

   iii.   Prophecy

B. Gifts of Revelation (Hearing)

    i.   Discernment (of spirits)

    ii.   Word of Knowledge

    iii.   Word of Wisdom

C. Gifts of Manifestation (Miracles)

    i.   Faith

    ii.   Healing

    iii.   Working of Miracles

He does not give the same gift to everyone; He distributes to each one of us as He pleases. This eliminates pride and discontent because God is the one who gives the gifts. He knows exactly why He gives each one of these special gifts to whom He chooses; the gifts are not given because of spirituality as the Corinthians believed. They highly regarded speaking in tongues, thinking that the more one speaks in tongues, the more spiritual he/she was. Perhaps this is why Paul started naming the intellectual gifts and ended with the emotional ones. God also does this so that no man is independent; we need the gifts of each other thus bringing the interdependence and unity among believers.

To teach this concept, Paul made an awesome comparison between the natural and spiritual body in 1Corinthians 12:14-21, "For the body is not one member, but many. If the foot says, "Because I am not a hand, I am not *a part* of the body," it is not, for this reason, any the less *a part* of the body. And if the ear says, "Because I am not an eye, I am not *a part* of the body," it is not, for this reason, any the less *a part* of the body. If the whole body were an eye, where would the hearing be? If the whole were hearing, where would the sense of smell be? But now God has placed the members, each one of them, in the body, just as He desired. If they were all one member, where would the body be? But now there are many members, but one body. And the eye cannot say to the hand, "I have no need of you"; or again the head to the feet, "I have no need of you."

Paul was teaching that the human body is one of diversity yet one of unity; it is one unit with several parts. Believers are different and each of us should perform different functions yet altogether we form the fully functional Body of Christ. Would you say that the foot is insignificant because it is not the ear? Consider some uses of the feet – to stand, to walk, to kick, to jump, to skip, to run, to climb, to dance, and so forth, but the brain must send the message to tell the feet what to do. Similarly, if you think of the many uses of each body part, you will cherish them individually. Sometimes it is when we lose one part of the body that we really recognize how important that part was. If the whole body was the ear, how would we survive? So, to with the Body of Christ; if everyone has the same gift, how would it function effectively?

You may be saying to yourself, "Where do I fit in all of this? I am not gifted like person 'x' and I feel inferior." Well hear ye the Word of the Lord: 1Corinthians 12:22-25 tells us, "On the contrary, it is much truer that the members of the body which seem to be weaker are necessary; and those *members* of the body which we deem less honorable, on these we bestow more abundant honor, and our less presentable members become much more presentable, whereas our more presentable members have no need *of it.* But God has *so* composed the

Body, giving more abundant honor to that *member* which lacked, so that there may be no division in the body, but *that* the members may have the same care for one another."

Christians who seem to have fewer essential functions in the Body of Christ are actually indispensable, quite like the physical body. The kidney, liver and other internal parts don't look as strong as the feet or arms, but we cannot live without any of them. These organs do not show themselves on the outside, but they still carry out their functions. God has combined all the differing members of the body into an organic structure and as a result, we must appreciate all the members. They are all interdependent! In the same sense, you may feel invaluable to the Body of Christ but if you understand the teaching brought about by Paul, you will know that you are most valuable.

Can the church say that it has no need for cleaners? Have you ever considered the importance of a cleaner? Can the church say it has no need for ushers? Think of any church duty which we label as basic then list what it accomplishes. Your church duty may not be elegant or attractive, but it is vital to the Body of Christ. One gives to another what is needed and receives in return, the help which only that member can give. The organs that we don't see like the brain, heart, lungs or the spleen can cause a fatality if they are not cared for. When one goes bad, the entire body feels the hurt. Paul puts it like this, "And if one member suffers, all the members suffer with it; if *one* member is honored, all the members rejoice with it," (1Corinthians 12:26). An ear-ache or a fever can affect the entire body and so is the Body of Christ. Yes, we are all distinct and separate, but all form the Body and are so crucially linked together that what affects one member, affects all.

Types of Services

Service for God takes many forms. It may take a form of a religious act or simply some act of kindness. Christians should serve each other as Peter puts it in 1Peter 4:10-11, "As each one has received a gift, minister it to one another, as good stewards of the manifold grace of God. If anyone speaks, *let him speak* as the oracles of God. If anyone ministers, *let him do it* as with the ability which God supplies, that in all things God may be glorified through Jesus Christ, to whom belong the glory and the dominion forever and ever. Amen."

Each of us as believers has received at least one spiritual gift from God. These gifts are a blessing from God. We are to be good stewards of His manifold grace towards us. Jesus was the first to teach about kind acts. Matthew 25:35-40 declares, "For I was hungry and you gave Me food; I was thirsty and you gave Me drink; I was a stranger and you took Me in; I *was* naked and you clothed Me; I was sick and you visited Me; I was in prison and you came to Me. Then the righteous will answer Him, saying, 'Lord, when did we see You hungry and feed *You,* or thirsty and give *You* drink? When did we see You a stranger and take *You* in, or naked and clothe *You?* Or when did we see You sick, or in prison, and come to You?' And the King will answer and say to them, 'Assuredly, I say to you, inasmuch as you did *it* to one of the least of these My brethren, you did *it* to Me.''

I know there is a deeper understanding of these verses of Scripture but in their simplest form, I want to draw your attention to the acts of kindness. There are many services Christians can offer here on earth using these verses. Hunger and thirst – look at your neighborhood to see the many who are shut-in, sick and underprivileged; some go to bed on an empty stomach. Is there any way we can help to alleviate their pain and suffering? Yes, we can do it on an individual or a group level. Take breakfast, lunch or dinner to one of them and you can also do it on a community level.

So much food is being wasted and yet some yearn for a bowl of soup, a cup of tea, a loaf of bread, some sugar, rice, flour, etc. Even with strangers, we can help; we can accommodate a missionary, evangelist, pastor, brother or sister. It may be someone who needs lodging for a short time or a contribution to their trip. You may not have money, but you may be able to bake a cake that will last them a couple days, etc. We see the reward of the Shunamite woman in 2Kings 4:8-36, she was so hospitable that she built a room for the servant of God, Elisha, and fed him joyfully. She didn't do it once but continually and what was her reward? God healed her of her bareness, and she bore a son.

The writer of Hebrews 13:2 encourages us to entertain strangers, "Do not forget to entertain strangers, for by so *doing* some have unwittingly entertained angels." Yes, my fellow Christian friends do not be afraid to invite people to your homes. A person may be attending a church service and do not know where their next meal is coming from. Invite a bachelor or a single sister, an elderly or a poor person; this speaks volumes to the individual. We can offer clothes; check your wardrobe and look at the clothes collecting dust, rotting, etc. See how many pairs of shoes you have and think of how many you have not worn for the year thus far. Check those too small or too large to fit. Some people would see it as a luxury!

Even in the church, you can have a closet or in your yard and invite the needy to come. For those who are sick, a home or hospital visit means a lot; for you to take time off your regular schedule to spend time with them will make the world of difference in their lives. There you can give hope through the Word of God and offer prayer; you can show compassion by relieving the pain and suffering for a short while. You can take the medication, water, food, etc. to the person or even assist their children. You may have a passion for a specific group of people; follow your heart to affect their lives. For instance, if you have the opportunity to go to the prison, please do not hesitate. Prison ministry is awesome! It can begin a second chance in life for many. Your word of encouragement in a dry and desperate season can get anyone back on track.

Let us all offer hope to the hopeless, peace to the troubled, healing to the hurting, and comfort to the mourning. Let us do it to those who are among us and ultimately it will be to Jesus. Examine the earthly ministry of Jesus; He specialized in these areas! The Bible has many examples of people who merely showed acts of kindness but made a great difference in the Body of Christ. One such woman is recorded in the book of Acts 9:36-41, "At Joppa there was a certain disciple named Tabitha, which is translated Dorcas. This woman was full of good works and charitable deeds which she did. But it happened in those days that she became sick and died. When they had washed her, they laid *her* in an upper room. And since Lydda was near Joppa, and the disciples had heard that Peter was there, they sent two men to him, imploring *him* not to delay in coming to them. Then Peter arose and went with them. When he had come, they brought *him* to the upper room. And all the widows stood by him weeping, showing the tunics and garments which Dorcas had made while she was with them. But Peter put them all out and knelt down and prayed. And turning to the body he said, "Tabitha, arise." And she opened her eyes, and when she saw Peter she sat up. Then he gave her *his* hand and lifted her up; and when he had called the saints and widows, he presented her alive."

Dorcas was well known for her kind deeds. She made clothes for the poor but one day she died suddenly and those who were present sent to call Peter urgently. Upon his arrival, Peter found all the widows there crying bitterly as they showed him the pieces, she made for them. Do you know what happened? A miracle took place! Peter prayed for her and God brought her back to life. God rewards our kindness. You may also recall the story of Hezekiah when the prophet Isaiah told him that God sent him to tell Hezekiah that he would die. Upon hearing the news, Hezekiah prayed to the Lord, telling God about his good deeds and God truly heard and rewarded him, adding fifteen more years to his life (2Kings 20:1-6).

The list of services mentioned in the Bible is almost inexhaustible, but I would like you to study the following examples and see where you may fit in. Your gift may be primary or secondary. Primary gifts are mentioned in Romans 12, 1Corinthians 12 and 14, and Ephesians 4. Secondary gifts appear in 1Corinthians 7, 13 and 14, 1Peter 4, and Ephesians 3. It is interesting to note that after the outpouring of the

Spirit in Acts 2 that the gifts were distributed. It is only to demonstrate that we need the power of God to properly utilize the gifts that were given to us. They go hand in hand!

You can examine a few of them in the book of Acts such as the gifts of tongues (2:6), interpretation of tongues (2:8-11), preaching/exhortation (2:14 and 5:33), teaching (2:42), signs/miracles (2:43, 3:6 and 5:12), mercy (2:45 and 5:34), giving (5:32), discernment (5:3), faith (3:6), healing (5:15), and intercession (5:29). We can continue to see the gifts of the Spirit in action throughout the New Testament. Now that you have a good understanding of the various gifts or services you can be engaged in; I hope you see that there is no excuse for you not to be serving the Body of Christ.

The last service that God left for us before receiving His Son into glory is found in Matthew 28:19, "Go therefore and make disciples of all the nations, baptizing them in the name of the Father and the Son and the Holy Spirit." This simply means to share your beliefs with others. To convince and persuade them that Christianity is the only way to heaven. Basically, this is why you are called a believer and you will need your gift(s) to do this effectively. Jesus is waiting on us! Matthew 9:37 says, "Then He said to His disciples, 'The harvest truly is plentiful, but the laborers are few.'" Will you be a laborer today? Can you share your faith with your family, friends, neighbors, workers, and colleagues? Yes, you can begin the Lord's service right there.

The apostle Paul said in Ephesians 2:10, "For we are His workmanship, created in Christ Jesus for good works, which God prepared beforehand so that we would walk in them." God made each one of us for a special purpose. We are a masterpiece of God! He created us for good works; although good works in itself does not save us but when we are saved, we need to perform good works (James 2: 14-26). From creation, your good work has been outlined for you. Have you started? If not, it's time to begin. How much did Paul understand his calling? Acts 20:24 says, "But I do not consider my life of any account as dear to myself, so that I may finish my course and the ministry which I received from the Lord Jesus, to testify solemnly of the gospel of the grace of God."

Paul got this calling from the first day of his conversion in Acts 9:15, "But the Lord said to him, 'Go, for he is a chosen instrument of Mine, to bear My name before the Gentiles and kings and the sons of Israel.'" Paul carried his assignment with first class honor. He was zealous, motivated, and changed from day one until the end. How remarkable he puts it in 2Timothy 4:7, "I have fought the good fight, I have finished the course, I have kept the faith." Paul looked back at his thirty years of labor and was well satisfied. He was a good steward! This begs the question, how long have you been in the faith? Some of us longer than Paul but have you started? Are you satisfied thus far? Jesus stressed the importance of doing your task now by saying, "I must work the works of Him who sent Me as long as it is day; night is coming when no one can work." (John 9:4).

May God help you function effectively in the Body of Christ. It may be that you are the ear or the nose or the kidney. Find which part you are in the Body. You are useful! Do not cause the body to function abnormally because you are not functioning well or at all. God is counting on you! Will you respond? I encourage you to answer the call today. Peter was an unlearned man and he was the greatest evangelist among the disciples. You have what it takes! The Holy Spirit will enable you. Launch out today!

Chapter 3
God is a God of Excellence

God's call comes unmistakably plain to everyone. God is a God of order, but the Bible has countless examples of times when God uses extra-ordinary people to do His will. Sometimes you may hear this is the work of a woman and not a man. I am not trying to discredit men, nor trying to push a feminist agenda but I have seen God use anyone or thing available to do His will. God has done things against the very law of nature. Joshua 10:12&13) states, "Then spake Joshua to the Lord in the day when the Lord delivered up the Amorites before the children of Israel, and he said in the sight of Israel, Sun, stand thou still upon Gibeon; and thou, Moon, in the valley of Ajalon. And the sun stood still, and the moon stayed, until the people had avenged themselves upon their enemies. Is not this written in the book of Jasher? So, the sun stood still in the midst of heaven, and hasted not to go down about a whole day."

God truly, divinely prolonged the day so that Joshua could complete the battle. God will always be God and does what pleases Him. In 2Kings 20:9-11 Isaiah said, "Isaiah said, "This shall be the sign to you from the Lord, that the Lord will do the thing that He has spoken: shall the shadow go forward ten steps or go back ten steps?" So, Hezekiah answered, "It is easy for the shadow to decline ten steps; no, but let the shadow turn backward ten steps." Isaiah the prophet cried to the Lord, and He brought the shadow on the stairway back ten steps by which it had gone down on the stairway of Ahaz." (See also Isaiah 38:8). Again, we see God changing the law of nature to do His pleasure.

Don't you agree there isn't anything more extra-ordinary than for God to use His children in any capacity that He wants? In the book of Numbers, there is a fascinating yet scary account of a conversation between Balaam and a donkey. This is something to ponder upon! Numbers 22:27-30 "When the donkey saw the angel of the Lord, she lay down under Balaam; so Balaam was angry and struck the donkey with his stick. And the Lord opened the mouth of the donkey, and she said to Balaam, "What have I done to you, that you have struck me these three times?" Then Balaam said to the donkey, "Because you have made a mockery of me! If there had been a sword in my hand, I would have killed you by now." The donkey said to Balaam, "Am I not your donkey on which you have ridden all your life to this day? Have I ever been accustomed to do so to you?" And he said, "No."

God uses what is present and available to do His work! He could have just opened Balaam's eye at first to see the angel, but he chose to use the donkey. A donkey was given the power to speak to Balaam, rebuking him for his inhumane treatment. This unusual encounter is also recorded in 2Peter 2:16. How much more can he use us humans? God is so amazing! Truly His ways are not ours, nor His thoughts are ours (Isaiah 55:9). His ways and thoughts are so far out of the box. Every time I read the Bible, I see a God without boundary, class, race or gender. He does not hold to norm because He proves himself over and over that He is God without limitations. Most men and women God has used are usually people the world looked down on. But God has always been delighted in using ordinary people- the poor, downtrodden, and outcast to achieve an extra-ordinary purpose.

That does not mean He does not use the mighty. 1Corinthians 1:26-29 "For consider your calling, brethren, that there were not many wise according to the flesh, not many mighty, not many noble; but God has chosen the foolish things of the world to shame the wise, and God has chosen the weak things of the world to shame the things which are strong, and the base things of the world and the despised God has chosen, the things that are not, so that He may nullify the things that are, so that no man may boast before God." He does not often choose philosophers, nor statesmen nor orators, nor people of great wealth and power to carry the gospel message but here are a few such persons that He did use.

Esther

She was a young Jewish girl who lived in Persia during the reign of Xerxes, where she was chosen to be queen in a contest. During that time Haman succeeded to allow the king to sign a decree to exterminate the Jewish population. But Esther was persuaded by her cousin Mordecai to foil the plan. She was used by God to save the Jewish nation. (Esther 8) Are you saying that you are too young to do Gods work?

Gideon

God called him to save Israel from the yearly reign of the Midianites (Judges 6:1-6). However, he was a coward, a fearful man. Three times he had an inquiry of God, to show him a miraculous sign in each instance to confirm it was really God (Judges 6:33-40). With three hundred men he conquered the Midianites. Are you saying that you are too afraid to do God's work?

Moses

He was a murderer; he slew an Egyptian and fled to the desert. He was later called by God after forty years to deliver the Israelites from bondage. What was his excuse? He could not speak. He was stammering. God used him mightily to bring freedom to his people. (Exodus 4:1-9, 30, 10-14, 7:12) Are you saying that you are not eloquent enough?

Simon Peter

He was merely a fisherman when God called him. He never studied in any Jewish religious college, yet he developed skills in preaching and teaching. He became one of the greatest apostles and evangelist in his time. He was the leader and spokesperson (Mark 1:36-37, 10:27-28). This same unlearned man wrote two epistles. Are you saying that you were a vagabond and do not feel worthwhile?

Rahab

Before Joshua opened his attack on Canaan, he sent two men to spy out the first city they would meet, Jericho. There, the men met Rahab, a prostitute. She protected the spies from Israelite authorities and in return, she and her family were protected when the Israelites attacked Jericho (Joshua 2:1-14). She became the mother of Boaz and later the ancestor of Jesus Christ (Matt 1:1&5-6). Imagine from a harlot to such a great height. Isn't that incredible? Are you saying that your past is too messed up?

David

He was the youngest of Jesse's sons. After the failure of Saul as king, God wanted a replacement. Samuel the prophet, was sent to the house of Jesse to anoint the king. Samuel called out all the sons of Jesse that he thought in his own fleshy eyes might be qualified to become the king, but God gave approval to none. He then inquired of Jesse if he had any other sons. Almost as an afterthought Jesse sent for little David who was at the time tending his sheep. Who would have guessed that he was the chosen one (1Samuel 13:14, 15:28 & 16:11-14)? The little shepherd boy was chosen above all other men in Israel including his brothers. If you think you are unqualified to be used of God, start changing your mindset. David became a musician, a very skillful one. He also became a psalmist and wrote many of the psalms that we sing today. David became the greatest king of Israel. Are you saying that you are too young or unqualified?

Deborah

She was a judge in Israel during the time of the judges. She was also a prophetess. Deborah led a great victory for God's people along with Barak against Sisera. God chose Deborah to judge his people (Judges 4:4) Are you saying you are a woman and that's not your place?

Abraham

He came from a country where the people worshipped idols. God called Abraham when he was seventy-five (75) years old. God promised him a son but it was not accomplished until twenty-five (25) years later when he was a hundred (100). Through this son, he became father of all nations (Matt 3:9 & John 8:37) because he accepted God's promise by faith, he is also the spiritual father of all who accepts God's promise by faith. A childless man became the father of all; God knows our inadequacies. Are you saying that you are too old?

Joseph

The story of Joseph is a fascinating one. He was Jacob's eleventh son, born of Rachel. Jealousy grew among his brothers because he was his father's favorite. His brothers sold him to traders who took him to Egypt. Joseph ended up in prison in Egypt although he was completely innocent. Joseph was also accused of trying to rape the king's wife. Because of his God-given wisdom in his ability to interpret dreams, he warned the king about a great famine which would come upon the land and advised him how to prepare for it. Joseph became the head of the food program and later governor of all Egypt (Genesis 41:1-45). So, you see, he went from a pit to a prison and then to governor. Are you allowing circumstances to stop you from doing God's work? Your best is yet to come.

The woman at the well

One of the greatest evangelists in Bible times was this woman at the well (John 4). She had been married about five times and was living with a man who was not her husband. After she met Jesus, she ran to the village and told the villagers of her encounter with him. Many followed and believed in the Lord Jesus Christ. The twelve disciples were on the scene all day long and not one of them had led a single soul to the Lord. Are you saying that you were an adulterer, fornicator or even a prostitute and that there is no place for you because everybody knows your story?

You are valuable in the eyes of God. Your mess becomes a message of importance once you allow Jesus to reign over your heart and life.

Dr. Miles Munroe

He was born and raised in the Bahamas but became internationally famous. He was just a regular school teacher but availed himself to God. He wrote about sixty-nine (69) books. He became a master teacher in the word of God, a great pastor, counselor and motivational speaker. His gift brought him before kings, queens, prime ministers, governors and presidents. He addressed the corporate world of business, churches, and people from every walk of life. He became a world changer! Consider his famous quote today, "When God looks at you, He sees things everybody else ignores."

My personal testimony

I was born and raised in a small village on the small island of St. Lucia. In 1979, I accepted the Lord as personal Savior. From the inception of my Christian journey, I served God with zeal. I always had a desire to do service for my Master in whatever capacity that

I was allowed to by my pastor. Since I was a teacher by profession, I started to teach the children's Sunday school class. Then later, I was moved to teach the adult class. However, within this time I never ceased to do menial work in the church. I collected song books and cleaned the church after the Sunday service in preparation for the evening service. I took pleasure in cleaning the sanctuary of God with other older women every weekend.

During my school vacation, I would assist in cleaning the church yard. In fact, any opportunity to do God's work which presented itself, I would avail myself. After many years, I was appointed as a deaconess and the church's treasurer. Again, I did my best! I always believed God's work should be done with honor. Unfortunately, there was a decision in our administrative staff in 1997 where I was asked to hold the top position of the church until things were resolved. This came as a great shock to me. A woman at the helm of my church was so unpopular back then and I had never been given an opportunity to preach before. I had never taught a Bible study class either. My only experience then was to lead a prayer meeting.

My first attempt was for three months and then it was prolonged to six months. I was in a dilemma! I wanted to give up, yet my inner spirit was saying you can't just scatter the people like this. Like King David, I had a survey done, more of a secret ballot to determine who the congregation wanted to lead them and surprisingly, by far I had the most support. I can still remember vividly, before the election I had a dream. In the dream, I saw a particular Scripture and as soon as I awoke, I quickly went to the bible to check the content. It was 2Corinthians 10:18 which says, "For it is not he who commends himself that is approved, but he whom the Lord commends."

I had never given any in-depth thought to this verse before, so I used Bible commentaries to unleash the revelation there. It is taken to mean, that self-commendation does not move God. Rather, He blesses the work, souls are saved, souls are established in the faith, and churches are planted when God approves you. There must be the Lord's commendation of someone's ministry for it to flourish.

Although I became a little more comfortable with the idea, lots of questions, fears, and doubts remained. One day a preacher came to the church and ministered from Galatians 3:28, "There is neither Jew nor Greek, there is neither slave nor free man, there is neither male nor female; for you are all one in Christ Jesus."

There were distinctions between these classes as in Deuteronomy 7:6, 14:1-2 but because of Jesus, all have become the same level; all differences disappeared. There is no preference whether you are free, a slave, a Jew, Gentile, male or female. Although I know it basically speaks of our heavenly position and not actually our earthly position, He was further confirming to me that He can use any of the classes mentioned for His glory. This concept is also found in Acts 10:34-35 "Opening his mouth, Peter said: "I most certainly understand now that God is not one to show partiality, but in every nation the man who fears Him and does what is right is welcome to Him."

I was therefore convinced without a shadow of a doubt that God called me to pastor the work. I am not making a case for or against male and female pastors because God's orders have always been for men to lead but the example mentioned earlier also shows that he uses even animals to carry out His work. I am delighted to serve him in the capacity of a pastor and God delights in bringing something from nothing. Yes, he uses us even when we do not have connections in education, the right background, finances, or any other advantageous points. All God needs is you! He will not share His glory with no other man. In fact, there is nothing you can contribute to bring to pass the call of God upon your life.

The apostle Paul was an educated man, who was perfect by the world's standard. He was a respected Pharisee, trained under Gamaliel, he was of the tribe of Benjamin, a Hebrew of Hebrews. He was a law-abiding citizen and he upheld the Law of Moses to the extent of being righteous and blameless. His conclusion in Philippians 3:7-8, "But whatever things were gain to me, those things I have counted as loss for the sake of Christ. More than that, I count all things to be loss in view of the surpassing value of knowing Christ Jesus my Lord, for whom I have suffered the loss of all things and count them but rubbish so that I may gain Christ." Paul did not rely on any of his worldly qualifications when he was called. God called without any recourse of anything he did. So, don't feel intimidated by anything!

Availability is what God is looking for. Start somewhere! God is the qualifier! The Bible says that Peter was an unlearned man, but he was the spokesman for the twelve apostles. He preached his first fiery message on the day of Pentecost and three thousand (3000) souls were saved. God loves to deal with the unassuming persons who are available to Him so that He can get the glory. In the past, God has used mighty men and women filled with issues and inconsistencies, imperfections and challenges, to do great work for him. People the world look down on or condemn are the target for God so that no flesh can glory in His handiwork.

God will find these unique people to achieve an extraordinary purpose. For example, Moses who stammered was used to save Israel. David went from an adulterer and murderer to become the greatest king in Israel, a man after God's own heart. Rahab, a prostitute was used to serve a nation. God used Esther, a young captor in Israel to save the Jewish nation of Israel. He used Paul who was a murderer to make him the writer of most of the epistles and the list goes on. Do not be derailed from the path of your destiny by accepting criticism. Once God is in it, go for it! I would like to encourage you according to the Lord's blessing on Joshua. "Have I not commanded you? Be strong and courageous! Do not tremble or be dismayed, for the Lord your God is with you wherever you go." (Joshua 1:9).

Chapter 4
Spiritual Power:
Vital for Effective Service

The Holy Spirit has all the qualities to help you succeed if you are willing to work for God. God has always included the Holy Spirit in everything He has done from creation. The Holy Spirit was part of creation as Genesis 1:2 shows "The earth was formless and void, and darkness was over the surface of the deep, and the Spirit of God was moving over the surface of the waters." What is the function of the Holy Spirit within the Christian church? The spirit is the renewed presence of God.

In the Old Testament days, the presence of God was normally experienced in Israel through the tabernacle in the wilderness and later the temple In Jerusalem. Exodus 33:14-16 declares, "And He said, 'My presence shall go with you, and I will give you rest.' Then he said to Him, 'If Your presence does not go with us, do not lead us up from here. For how then can it be known that I have found favor in Your sight, I and Your people? Is it not by Your going with us, so that we, I and Your people, may be distinguished from all the other people who are upon the face of the earth?'"

Isaiah 6:1-4 also states, "In the year of King Uzziah's death I saw the Lord sitting on a throne, lofty and exalted, with the train of His robe filling the temple. Seraphim stood above Him, each having six wings: with two he covered his face, and with two he covered his feet, and with two he flew. And one called out to another and said, 'Holy, Holy, Holy, is the Lord of hosts, the whole earth is full of His glory.' And the foundations of the thresholds trembled at the voice of him who called out, while the temple was filling with smoke."

In another incident, where the people of God were celebrating the return of the Ark of the Covenant, the presence of God was so powerful that not even the priests could function in their duties. 1Kings 8:10-11 declares, "It happened that when the priests came from the holy place, the cloud filled the house of the Lord, so that the priests could not stand to minister because of the cloud, for the glory of the Lord filled the house of the Lord." God did not only offer His presence in the sanctuary in the Old Testament but came mightily upon His chosen people and empowered them for His service. Consider a few selected ones below:

Othniel

Judges 3:10 records "The Spirit of the Lord came upon him, and he judged Israel. When he went out to war, the Lord gave Cushan-rishathaim, king of Mesopotamia into his hand, so that he prevailed over Cushan-rishathaim." The Spirit of the Lord came upon Othniel to deliver God's people.

Jephthah

Judges 11:29 records "Now the Spirit of the Lord came upon Jephthah, so that he passed through Gilead and Manasseh; then he passed through Mizpah of Gilead, and from Mizpah of Gilead he went on to the sons of Ammon."

Samson

Judges 14:6&9 records "The Spirit of the Lord came upon him mightily, so that he tore him as one tears a young goat though he had nothing in his hand; but he did not tell his father or mother what he had done." And "Then the Spirit of the Lord came upon him mightily, and he went down to Ashkelon and killed thirty of them and took their spoil and gave the changes of clothes to those who told the riddle. And his anger burned, and he went up to his father's house."

Saul

1 Samuel 10:6&7 records "Then the Spirit of the Lord will come upon you mightily, and you shall prophesy with them and be changed into another man. It shall be when these signs come to you, do for yourself what the occasion requires, for God is with you."

David

1 Samuel 16:13 records "Then Samuel took the horn of oil and anointed him in the midst of his brothers; and the Spirit of the Lord came mightily upon David from that day forward. And Samuel arose and went to Ramah."

What is the commonality among all these experiences with the different men of God? The spirit endued them with power. You see from creation the Holy Spirit has been a moving force, representing the power of the Godhead. So, we understand that the origin of the spirit originates in the Old Testament. When people of the Old Testament saw some of the remarkable demonstrations of the power of God, they called that power by the Hebrew word "Ruach." This word indicated to them, something that was powerful and inevitable.

Zechariah 4:6 shows us "Then he said to me, "This is the word of the Lord to Zerubbabel saying, 'Not by might nor by power, but by My Spirit,' says the Lord of hosts." 2Samuel 23:2 tells us, "The Spirit of the Lord spoke by me, And His word was on my tongue." Zechariah 7:12 says, "They made their hearts like flint so that they could not hear the law and the words which the Lord of hosts had sent by His Spirit through the former prophets; therefore, great wrath came from the Lord of hosts."

The power of the Holy Spirit enables the work to be done easier because it is not by human energy or power. God promised that a day was coming when not only selected people would get the privilege of being endued with the Spirit but all God's people regardless of status, sex, age or nationality would have God's Spirit poured out upon them. In the Old Testament, a number of prophesies were brought by godly men who were prophets, speaking of the Spirit in full force.

Joel 2:28-29 states, "It will come about after this: That I will pour out My Spirit on all mankind; And your sons and daughters will prophesy, your old men will dream dreams, your young men will see visions. Even on the male and female servants, I will pour out My Spirit in those days." This prophesy was partially fulfilled in Acts 2:16-21. All barriers were to be broken- gender, age, nationality. The outpouring of the Spirit was meant for every single believer without prejudice.

The Spirit in the New Testament

There were no miracles recorded during Jesus' first thirty (30) years of his life. After he was baptized by John, then the Holy Spirit came upon him.

Mark 1:10-11 declares "Immediately coming up out of the water, He saw the heavens opening, and the Spirit like a dove descending upon Him; and a voice came out of the heavens: "You are My beloved Son, in You I am well-pleased." Luke 4:18 says "The Spirit of the Lord is upon Me, Because He anointed Me to preach the gospel to the poor. He has sent Me to proclaim release to the captives, and recovery of sight to the blind, to set free those who are oppressed," This was also prophesized in Isaiah 61:1-3.

When we carefully examine the work, Jesus left for us to do as Christians, it is encapsulated in Luke 4:16-18:

1. Bringing the good news of salvation to the poor.
2. Building up the brokenhearted.
3. Proclaiming liberty to those held captive by sin.
4. Opening the prison and the eyes of those who are bound.

Jesus was anointed with the Holy Spirit at His baptism to begin His earthly ministry. How much more do we need this anointing to do our Godly ministry here on earth? Jesus is our perfect example of anointed ministry! We are blessed with spiritual gifts but there must be a supernatural power to enable us to operate each one of them effectively and this power is undoubtedly the power of the Holy Spirit.

The baptism with the Holy Spirit

The same power that Jesus had on earth is for us today. "And behold, I am sending forth the promise of My Father upon you; but you are to stay in the city until you are clothed with power from on high." (Luke 24:49). The apostles had to wait for the coming of the Holy Spirit at Pentecost. They would then be endued/clothed with divine power to bear witness to the risen Christ. The apostle Paul encouraged his followers to appreciate the power of God in every sphere, that God has ordained for us to do. Ephesians 1:19 reminds us "And what is the surpassing greatness of His power toward us who believe. These are in accordance with the working of the strength of His might."

As Christians, we must take advantage of the availability of the power of God. John got a revelation of that power in Luke 3:16 'John answered and said to them all, "As for me, I baptize you with water; but One is coming who is mightier than I, and I am not fit to untie the thong of His sandals; He will baptize you with the Holy Spirit and fire." The church really started in the book of Acts and I would like you to note that the subject of the spirit to empower God's people to serve effectively began from the first chapter. Jesus wanted the disciples to get it right! The Holy Spirit must empower Christians before they are sent forth, so that they will not serve in and of themselves but in His might.

In Acts 1:4-5 the writer reminded us of what Jesus told them, "Gathering them together, He commanded them not to leave Jerusalem, but to wait for what the Father had promised, 'Which,' He said, 'you heard of from Me; for John baptized with water, but you will be baptized with the Holy Spirit not many days from now.'" The writer then reminded them of the purpose of that power, "but you will receive power when the Holy Spirit has come upon you; and you shall be My witnesses both in Jerusalem, and in all Judea and Samaria, and even to the remotest part of the earth." (Acts 1:8). Notice that Jesus did not just send them to serve without empowering them, but they had to tarry for it.

Jesus knew the challenges that faced them in witnessing or serving Him. He also wanted to equip them to face the entire world regardless of race, color, sex, or status. First, they had to begin in Jerusalem, which was then a city filed with hatred, violence and persecution. Additionally, that was the place where Jesus was crucified. Then they had to be witnesses in Samaria, which was a half-Jewish population with whom Jesus had no dealings. From Samaria, they had to go to Judea, which was a strong Jewish population where Jerusalem was the chief city. Finally, they had to be witnesses in the uttermost part of the earth. There they had to go to the Gentiles worldwide.

So, you would understand like Jesus did, that the witnesses had to be strong, fearless and bold. These could not witness effectively without the endued power of the Holy Ghost. Then in Acts 2, we observed the real outpouring took place. Acts 2:1-4 tells us, "When the day of Pentecost had come, they were all together in one place. And suddenly there came from

heaven a noise like a violent rushing wind, and it filled the whole house where they were sitting. And there appeared to them tongues as of fire distributing themselves, and they rested on each one of them. And they were all filled with the Holy Spirit and began to speak with other tongues, as the Spirit was giving them utterance."

The onlookers were astonished but Peter reminded them that this is what was spoken of through the prophet Joel. He told them that the Lord had fulfilled His promise. He had poured out His spirit on all flesh who had come together, and whose hearts were in one accord. Many received the message and about three hundred (300) souls were saved because it was a message empowered by the Holy Spirit. Acts 2:37 recorded that the people were convinced in their hearts and then responded to the gospel. These disciples literally turned the world upside down because they were empowered to spread the good news. You may wonder why the church is ineffective in ministry. Simply put, too many people are satisfied with the outward physical baptism and not the inward, spiritual baptism.

You may be talented, highly skilled or educated but you need the spiritual power. The apostle Paul recognized and valued the power of the Holy Spirit when he made that bold declaration. Acts 2:4 states, "And they were all filled with the Holy Spirit and began to speak with other tongues, as the Spirit was giving them utterance." History tells us that the Apostle Paul was a well-educated man who studied under the philosopher, Gamaliel. However, he knew he could not depend on intellectualism, ambition, library, knowledge, psychology or theology. He acknowledged that preaching without the power of God kills, but the Spirit gives life. The spirit will open the stony hearts as in Acts 2:38. The power of God is needed in our preaching and teaching to slain sinners and fill our altars.

The apostle Paul said it well, "For I am not ashamed of the gospel, for it is the power of God for salvation to everyone who believes, to the Jew first and also to the Greek," (Romans 1:16). It began with the Holy Spirit in Acts 1:8. The Samaritans received this gift in Acts 8:14-17 and the Gentiles received this gift in Acts 10:44-46. Acts 6:1-7, gives an account of the growth of the church. The number of disciples was increasing, and the elders had little time to pray and study the word of God. The twelve apostles called a meeting to give advice and direction as to the way forward. The plan discussed was to select seven men to serve tables. These were called deacons.

I want you to notice that one of the qualifications to serve tables was to be filled with the

Spirit. Acts 6:3 says, "Therefore, brethren, select from among you seven men of good reputation, full of the Spirit and of wisdom, whom we may put in charge of this task." It is interesting to note that if deacons had to be filled with the Spirit to serve tables, how much more should the teachers, preachers, evangelists, worshippers, musicians etc. be filled with the Spirit. This same power is for us today! Ephesians 1:19-20 affirms, "And what is the surpassing greatness of His power toward us who believe. *These are* in accordance with the working of the strength of His might which He brought about in Christ when He raised Him from the dead and seated Him at His right hand in the heavenly *places.*"

Also, Romans 8:11 claims, "But if the Spirit of Him who raised Jesus from the dead dwells in you, He who raised Christ Jesus from the dead will also give life to your mortal bodies through His Spirit who dwells in you." Acts 2:38 proclaims, "Peter said to them, "Repent, and each of you be baptized in the name of Jesus Christ for the forgiveness of your sins;

and you will receive the gift of the Holy Spirit." Acts 2:39 tells us, "For the promise is for you and your children and for all who are far off, as many as the Lord our God will call to Himself." The Ephesians too received this gift as demonstrated in Acts 19:1-6.

The baptism with the Holy Spirit is a gift we do not have to work for. All we have to do is to receive the gift! Our heavenly father is ready to give you that gift. Receive it by faith! Live a holy life (sanctified), pray and praise God with expectation and you will be surprised to know how much He wanted to give you this precious gift to empower you for effective ministry.

In Ephesians 4:11, Jesus names the gifts. These are known as the Five-Fold Ministry: Apostles, Prophets, Evangelists, Pastors, and Teacher. In verse 12 of the same chapter, the purpose of the gifts is given.

1. To equip the saints
2. The saints then serve
3. The body is then built up

Notice the second purpose is to help the saints to serve. In this context serving means every form of spiritual service. As a result, there is a ministry for every believer. So, the five-fold ministry must perfect the saints for their ministry. As you go forth to use your gift which God has given to you, then you help the church to grow and expand. The five-fold ministry can't do all. You have a specific ministry, get up, rise up and do it. If you don't, then you hinder the work of God. Honestly, I don't believe you want to stand as a hindrance in the work of the lord.

In verse 13, Paul said this growth must continue till we all come to a state of unity, maturity and conformity. By no means can anyone of these be accomplished on earth. So, you must do service until the last breath. There was this famous evangelist called Shambach from the United States. Often after eighty years, people would ask him, "When are you retiring?" He would reply. "I don't know retiring. I know firing up." So, let's fire up and not retire from service especially when we have strength to do it.

George Miller, GochurchGo 1992. Revised 2001 RMI Publishing.

Permit me to share from the booklet written by George Miller, GochurchGo on the subject "God can use you." He spoke about eventful move of God when we as Christians avail ourselves to God whether by old, middle age or young. He reported the following testimonials.

1. Paul Yongi Cho came to build through the faithful witness of a young Christian girl. His ministry has touched the world.

2. Rich Stanley, the brother of the late "King of Rock" Elvis Presley, came to Christ through the witness of a young woman who was close to him and bold enough to say, "with all your money, you still need Jesus." He went to church with her, got saved and married her. They traveled together all over the world preaching the gospel.

3. Another young woman had been saved only for three months, when one day while out shopping the lord told her to pray for a sick woman in the shop. Eventually she did and god healed that woman. As a result, many members of the family of the woman who was healed were influenced for Christ.

4. Young Justin was only eleven years old, but was saved and knew it. His witness brought his mother to Christ and has a powerful effect on his father

5. Rich and Rosemary's marriage was finished. Their suitcases were packed in the hallway. It was the day of the Big Split. Two ordinary Christians were doing door-to-door work and

knocked at their door. As they shared the gospel with them, Rick and Mary surrendered to Jesus. Their lives were transformed by the power of God. Their marriage was saved. And now they both travel the world sharing Jesus.

6. After years of faithful praying by some of God's people, the Welch revival was started off by a few young Christian who began to obey God.

We love to read the experiences of the bible characters but if they had not availed themselves to God, they wouldn't be spiritual heroes and heroines today. Simple people who just obeyed God and moved. God used a donkey to speak. He will raise the rock if worshippers fail to arise.

Chapter 5
Consequences and Rewards

It has been established that a Christian's first call is to serve God. Jesus, during His earthly life, used lots of parables to teach His people. Parables helped people understand spiritual things from a natural point of view. One of the most powerful Scriptures found in the Bible to illustrate rewards and consequences of the work of God is the parable of the Ten Talents, which can be found in Matthew 25:14-30 and Luke 19:12-17. The parable illustrates the responsibility that rests upon us as the children of God, as we wait for Jesus' return. Christians were never called to a life of idleness. Our calling is one of occupancy and good stewardship meaning busy with God's work until His second coming. Let's see what there is to learn from the parable.

Matthew 25:14-15, "For *it is* just like a man, *about* to go on a journey, who called his own slaves and entrusted his possessions to them. To one he gave five talents, to another, two, and to another, one, each according to his own ability; and he went on his journey." The term talent was first used for a unit of weight which was equivalent to 75 pounds. Later, it was used as courage but in this parable, it also means an ability or gift. Jesus is a noble man who went to a far-off place to receive for Himself a kingdom and to return for His Church. This noble man wanted true servants but gave everyone a fair chance to work. He called all His servants and distributed the talents according to their ability.

This is the work of a just God who did not give to His servants any insurmountable task but to everyone in line with his own ability. This is real consideration! However, the distributor of the talents in the parable did not tell them when he was returning but he expected them to begin working right away. Just like Jesus! He expects us to be a part of His body and function efficiently in it. So, if you are the eye, you must be operating as an eye. He does not burden any of His servants with any task. Once you are enlisted in His army, there is a job you can do comfortably, once you choose to honor Him in this way. In the end, we will all be called upon to give an account of our stewardship.

After the long journey, the master returned, and the day of reckoning arrived when everyone would get his due. Matthew 25:16-18 relays to us that "Immediately the one who had received the five talents went and traded with them and gained five more talents. In the same manner, the one who *had received* the two *talents* gained two more. But he who received the one *talent* went away and dug *a hole* in the ground and hid his master's money." The man who had received five talents made a hundred percent gain, wasn't that great profit? Oh, he worked wisely! Who wouldn't be proud of such an employee? Think of it in the natural, there would be high praise for such a worker. Probably the employee of the year award or some great bonuses.

In the kingdom of God, we are business people as well; we are employed by the Most High God. We are supposed to find systems to make God's business work, grow and succeed. I ask this question, "How much benefit or profit do we give back to Him?" In the second case, the second servant was given two talents and he gained two more. Note he was given two and also doubled his profit. This was also a hundred percent increase. The servant was also worthy of great praise and recognition. The master perhaps would have given him an additional one next time because he was a good steward. Be reminded that each was given according to his ability. The master couldn't expect the second to make more gain than the first servant because that was his ability. He was pleased with him and gave him his warranted blessings.

Then, the third one was given one talent. What's your expectation? You may be expecting a double also but interestingly, the last servant did not even bother to try investing the talent. Instead, he accused and blamed the master. He said his master was hard and perhaps without consideration. He claimed that his master reaped where he had not sown and gathered where he had not scattered seed. To make it worse, he was fearful of him. As a result, he hid the talent not even considering using it somewhere it could gain interest. How did his master deal with him?

Matthew 25:26-30 reveals to us "But his master answered and said to him, 'You wicked, lazy slave, you knew that I reap where I did not sow and gather where I scattered no *seed*. Then you ought to have put my money in the bank, and on my arrival, I would have received my *money* back with interest. Therefore, take away the talent from him, and give it to the one who has the ten talents.' For to everyone who has, *more* shall be given, and he will have abundance; but from the one who does not have, even what he does have shall be taken away. Throw out the worthless slave into the outer darkness; in that place there will be weeping and gnashing of teeth."

His master did not accept his excuse. In fact, he called him wicked and lazy. The fact that he knew his master was hard, should have propelled him to think of making gains for his master. If he at least had gained one talent, the master would commend him because this was his ability. He had a poor, thoughtless excuse. So, I ask you again, what is your excuse? Shyness?

Carelessness? Idleness? Fear? Whatever it may be our Lord will say, its unacceptable. The master did not only rebuke his servant but took the talent from him and gave it to the one who had ten. Another law of Christ was fulfilled here.

Matthew 25:29 explains that, "For to everyone who has, more shall be given, and he will have an abundance; but from the one who does not have, even what he does have shall be taken away." The more a Christian does service for God, the more he is enabled to do so. It could also mean that you have money but can't manage it single handedly. You can give it to another Christian who may help you to invest in programs such as radio and television Christian programs, missionaries, elderly homes, feeding programs, etc. You will certainly make gains for your Master. Do not just allow your gifts and abilities or money, etc. to sit idly by. Our Lord is a good and loving Master. Do not treat it as the servant who was given the one talent.

The gist of the parable is that Jesus taught basically to admonish us that we do not just sit around, having salvation and waiting for His return. Whilst we wait, there is work to be done and since His return is nearer, we must be diligent, keen and so gracious. We must be engaged in service that produces results. Why are we occupied in our own business? We keep ourselves busy to be successful. Hebrews 6:10 admonishes us, "For God is not unjust so as to forget your work and the love which you have shown toward His name, in having ministered and in still ministering to the saints." Christians should not be slothful with the Lord's business.

Paul warns us in the way we do our earthly work far more than the work of God. Colossians 3:23-24 encourages us that "Whatever you do, do your work heartily, as for the Lord rather than for men, knowing that from the Lord you will receive the reward of the inheritance. It is the Lord Christ whom you serve." As Christians we must work from the heart and soul as unto the Lord, whether it be a prestigious or a loathsome task. All our work must be faithful in any task we do whether secular or sacred. In fact, God is keeping record of all that we do in the church, at home, at play or at work. Sometimes I don't seem to understand when a Christian is very vibrant and aggressive in his own business and so slack in the work of God. Jesus is the one who gives us the strength, health and yes, the very breath of life. He is the one who gives us the power to get wealth (Deuteronomy 8:18). Let us work for him!

Conclusion

To this end, I wish to encourage all my readers to take their walk with God seriously. Let us all partner with God in the wonderful work of reconciliation of lost souls back to Him and the edification of the Body of Christ. The truth of the matter is that God does not need any of us, He is self-sufficient and can do what He wants, when He wants and how He wants. Nevertheless, He offers us this awesome privilege to come alongside Him in accomplishing His work on this earth. Have we ever stopped to consider what debt we owe to God for salvation? God knew we would never be able to pay for such an invaluable gift so He has given it freely to men.

Consider with me the nature of God as a Master. God gave us life, gave us salvation, gave us the Holy Spirit to teach and guide, gave us gifts, abilities and talents, gives us daily strength and wisdom to use these, and if that wasn't enough, He rewards us for our work. Which boss in the cosmos could you ever fathom being so generous to his staff? Only God. Yet still, some of us fail to be grateful and give back to Him the one thing He deserves – a life of service to Him and others. This is the only real worship that is acceptable to God; one that flows out of a life surrendered to and serving Him. I pray that each reader will join me on this adventurous journey of completing God's work on this earth!